Also by Sarah A. Chrisman:

Historical Fiction:
First Wheel in Town
Love Will Find A Wheel
A Rapping at the Door
Delivery Delayed
A Trip and a Tumble

Non-fiction:
Victorian Secrets
This Victorian Life

Anthologies:
Love's Messenger
Words for Parting
A Christmas Wish
The Wheelman's Joy
True Ladies and Proper Gentlemen
Quotations of Quality

A Bouquet of Victorian Roses

19th-century Remarks, Poetry and Short Stories About the Queen of Flowers

Compiled and edited by
Sarah A. Chrisman

Sarah A. Chrisman

Introduction

Since Ancient times, the rose has been hailed as the supreme Queen of Flowers. Her beauty and fragrance evoke both romantic love and noble divinity. In the Victorian language of flowers each representative of the botanical family had meaning, but the rose held special pride of place.

In this collection of Victorian writings on roses the timeless fragrance of old blossoms is gathered for your enjoyment. The section titled, "Stray Petals" gathers together praise and remarks in short prose about our favorite flower, while in "Little Buds" we are treated to poetry redolent of roses. The best bouquets include fully blown roses, and in "Blossoms" we find three stories that each pivot around a different interpretation of the rose: rose as omen; rose as memory and reconciliation; rose as the sweetest epitome of romance.

Take up this bouquet, breathe deeply, and let its fragrance guide you backwards through the gate of Time's garden.

—*S.C.*

Index

Stray Petals

Little Buds

Blossoms

Stray Petals
Remarks About Roses

"The Queen of Flowers—so the Rose has been styled almost from time immemorial. And well it is named. Other flowers combine beauty and elegance of form, with fresh and brilliant colours. But to these, in the Rose, are added endless variety of colour, and form and habit, and a perfume so delightful as to make the Rose the most desirable of flowers."
—Thomas Affleck, 1851.
Southern Rural Almanac, October, 1851, p. 61.

***

"The Pagan Rose, was essentially the Rose of Triumph. The Rose graced every banquet, and crowned the heads of the revelers. Garlands of Roses decked the temples of their gods, and reddened all the way in the triumphs of their Heroes. The Rose, for them, wore the colors of a beautiful exultant joy in life for life's own sake..."
—E.V.B., 1885.
Dew of the Ever-Living Rose, 1885. pp. xv-xvi.

***

"The first Rose ever seen was said to have been given by the god of love to Harpocrates, the god of silence, to engage him not to divulge the amours of his mother Venus; and from hence the ancients made it a symbol of silence, and it became a custom to place a Rose above their heads, in their banqueting rooms, in order to banish restraint, as nothing there said would be repeated elsewhere; and from this practice originated the saying "sub rosa" (under the rose) when anything was to be kept secret."

—Henry Shaw, 1882.
The Rose: Historical and Descriptive, 1882, p. 7.

***

"One fable relates that Flora, having found the dead body of one of her favorite nymphs, whose beauty could only be equalled by her virtue, implored the assistance of all the Olympian deities to aid her in changing it into a flower, which all others should acknowledge to be their queen. Apollo lent the vivifying power of his beams, Bacchus bathed it in nectar, Vertumnus gave its perfume, Pomona its fruit, and Flora herself gave its diadem of flowers."

—S.B. Parsons, 1847.
The Rose: Its History, Poetry, Culture and Classification, 1847, p. 9.

***

"The word rose in the English tongue has certainly a pensive and lingering sound, suggestive of the dreamy warmth and light of a long summer day,—one of those summer days in which the queen rose revels and expands into surpassing beauty."
—Alexander Moore, 1871.
Good Health, 1871. p. 238.

***

"The oriental writers also represent the nightingale as sighing for the love of the Rose... "
—S.B. Parsons, 1847.
The Rose: Its History, Poetry, Culture and Classification, 1847, p. 10.

***

"What flower did she most resemble?... A rose! Certainly... strong, vigorous, self-asserting... yet shapely, perfect in outline and development, exquisite, enchanting in its never fully realized tints, yet compelling the admiration of every one, and recalling its admirers again and again by the unspoken

appeal of its own perfection—its unvarying radiance."
—John Habberton, 1876.
Helen's Babies, 1876, pp. 20—21.

***

"To paint this universal emblem of delicate splendor in its own hues, the pencil should be dipped in the tints of Aurora, when arising amidst her aerial glory. Human art can neither colour nor describe so fair a flower."
—Henry Shaw, 1882.
The Rose: Historical and Descriptive, 1882, p. 5.

***

"[W]hat superlative could heighten the love with which [the rose] is universally regarded?"
—Alexander Moore, 1871.
Good Health, 1871. p. 238.

***

"The ancients possessed, at a very early period, the luxury of roses, and the Romans brought it to perfection by covering with beds of these flowers the couches whereon their

guests were placed, and even the tables which were used for banquets; while some emperors went so far as to scatter them in the halls of their palace. At Rome, they were, at one time, brought from Egypt, in that part of the year when Italy could not produce them; but afterwards, in order to render these luxuries more easily attainable during the winter… their gardeners found the means of producing, in green-houses warmed by means of pipes filled with hot water, an artificial temperature, which kept roses and lilies in bloom until the last of the year."
—S.B. Parsons, 1847.
The Rose: Its History, Poetry, Culture and Classification, 1847, p. 14.

***

"Great joy has it been, at times, to see shining amid thorns, some full and perfect flower. A flower whose ripely rounded perfection, the changing seasons of the world can never mar…"
—E.V.B., 1885.
Dew of the Ever-Living Rose, 1885. p. xii.

***

"The rose is as near perfection as anything the earth can produce. Its color and its form are alike exquisite... and the emblem of eternity."
—Alexander Moore, 1871.
Good Health, 1871. p. 238.

***

"At midsummer, too, it is poetry to lie under the shade of a noble forest tree, and gaze upon the various forms of beauty displayed in the roses scattered about the lawn... This species of poetry cannot, however, be readily put upon paper; it is too etherial to pass under the press."
—S.B. Parsons, 1847.
The Rose: Its History, Poetry, Culture and Classification, 1847, p. 62.

***

"The rose is especially the flower of fairyland, of romance, of poetry."
—Alexander Moore, 1871.
Good Health, 1871. p. 238.

***

"It is a remarkable feature in the career of the Rose, that it appears always to have been exempt from those caprices of fashion which have from time to time affected the fortunes of other beautiful flowers —now exalting them into the objects of a mania, now consigning them to equally unreasoning neglect. Every one who has a taste for floral beauty admires the Rose..."
—W.D. Prior
Roses and Their Culture, 1878, p. 1.

***

"The conserve of any variety of roses is considered excellent in cases of cold or catarrh. It is prepared by bruising in a mortar the petals with their weight in sugar, and moistening them with a little rose-water, until the whole forms a homogenous mass. Some receipts prescribe powdered petals mixed with an equal part of sugar; others direct to use two layers of sugar and only one layer of pulverized petals."
—S.B. Parsons, 1847.
The Rose: Its History, Poetry, Culture and Classification, 1847, p. 52.

***

"The Rose, the emblem of beauty and the pride of Flora, reigns Queen of the flowers in every part of the globe, and the bards of all nations and languages have sung its praises. Yet, what poet has been able, or language sufficient to do justice to a plant that has been denominated the Daughter of Heaven, the glory of spring, the ornament of the earth? As it is the most common of all that compose the garland of Flora, so it is the most delightful."

—Henry Shaw, 1882.

The Rose: Historical and Descriptive, 1882, p. 4.

Meanings of Roses

From the Language and Sentiment of Flowers,
Hill's Manual, 1891.

Rosebud…Confession of love
Cinnamon rose… Without pretension
Hundred leaved rose [English rose]…
The graces
Austrian rose… Thou art all that is lovely
Rose leaf… I never trouble
Monthly rose… Beauty ever new
Moss rose… Superior merit; voluptuousness
Musk rose… Capricious beauty
Red rose… I love you
White rose… Silence
Wild single rose… Simplicity

A Recipe for Rose Cake

One-half cup white sugar, 1/2 cup red sugar, 1/2 cup butter, 1/2 cup milk, 2 cups flour, 1 teaspoon baking powder; flavor with rose. Beat the butter and sugar to a cream; then [add] the red sugar, milk and flour [and the baking powder]; whites of 6 eggs beaten to a froth the last thing. Bake in a slow oven.

—Mrs. M.W. Ellsworth, 1899.

Queen of the Household, 1899. p. 91.

Little Buds
Rose Poetry

Roses

"It is summer," says a fairy,
"Bring me tissue light and airy;
Bring me colors of the rarest,
Search the rainbow for the fairest—
Sea-shell pink and sunny yellow,
Kingly crimson, deep and mellow,
Faint red in Aurora beaming,
And the white in pure pearls gleaming;

"Bring me diamonds, shining brightly
Where the morning dew lies lightly;
Bring me gold dust, by divining
Where the humming-bird is mining;
Bring me sweets as rich as may be
From the kisses of a baby;—
With an art no fay discloses
I am going to make some roses."

—Mrs. M.F. Butts
St. Nicholas, July, 1880, p. 736.

The Child and the Rose

When stirring bud and songful bird
Brought gladness to the earth,
And spring-time voices first were heard
In low, sweet sounds of mirth;

A little child, with pleasant eyes,
Reclined in tranquil thought,
And, half communing with the skies,
His pretty fancies wrought.

He turned where, cased in robe of green,
A rose-bud met his eye,
And one faint streak the leaves between,
Rich in its crimson dye.

The warm light gathereth in the sky,
The bland air stirreth round,
And yet the child is lingering by,
Half-kneeling on the ground:

For broader grew that crimson streak,
Back folds the leaf of green,
And he in wonder, still and meek,
Watch'd all its opening sheen.

"'Tis done, 'tis done!" At length he cried,

With glad amazement wild;
The Rose, in new-created pride,
Had opened for the child.

O, had we hearts like thee, sweet boy,
To watch creative power,
We, too, should thrill with kindred joy
At every opening flower.

—E. Oakes Smith
*The Rose: Its History, Poetry, Culture and
Classification*, 1847, p. 68—69.

The First Rose of Summer

Shielded from harm in some warm sheltered
place,
Half fearful of the sun that calls it forth,
Dreading the bitter winds from east and north,
The first sweet rose of summer shows its face.
And lo! Such beauties in its youth we trace,
That its new-opening bud is dearer far
Than those more grandly perfect blossoms are

That later summer dowers with queenly grace,
So fair to see is maidenhood that goes
With half-unconscious steps upon the way
That marks her laughing childhood's happy
close;
For truth and purity are her array,
And, full of grace, like summer's first sweet
flower,
She reigns a queen long ere she knows her
power.

—George Weatherly
The Peterson Magazine, May, 1884, p. 434.

Little Rose

Beautiful rose, with fragrance sweet,
Why do you linger in silence there;
Wasting your scent and petals neat,
Flinging them all on the desert air?

Dear little rose, you are free from care,
Your quiet life is "short but sweet,"
Ah! Many have wished to molder where
The sunbeams kiss the sod at your feet!

—Lulu Lyon
The Peterson Magazine, June, 1884, p. 500.

Rose Leaves

These are leaves of my Rose,
Pink petals I treasure;
There is more than one knows
In these leaves of my Rose:
O the joys! O the woes!
They are quite beyond measure,
These are leaves of my Rose,
Pink petals I treasure.

—Austin Dobson
Dew of the Ever-Living Rose, p. 245.

Roses

In the world was one green nook I knew,
Full of Roses, red and white,
Reddest Roses summer ever grew,
Whitest Roses ever pearled with dew;
And their sweetness was beyond delight,
Was all love's delight.

—Augusta Webster
Dew of the Ever-Living Rose, p. 255.

Wild Roses

Afar o'er the Northern prairies
Wild roses are blooming to-day,
The air has a hint of their fragrance
O'er meadows of new-mown hay.

They blossom along the highways
In radiant pink and white,
And glorify all the byways
With petals of dawn's own light.

Of all the bloom of the prairies
The rose is the sweetest guest,
The gifts of the elves and the fairies,
To children who love it best.

Children who weave into garlands
These sprays of the Summer hour,
Nor dream that life hath aught sweeter
Than the humble prairie flower;

Nor know that in crowded cities
Eyes long for a glimpse once more
Of the sweet wild rose of the uplands,
Beloved, as in days of yore.

O roses sweet by the wayside,

Roses of white and of red,
Fair by the couch of the weary,
Fair by the face of the dead.

And fair in the palm of Summer
This coronal of the year,
With memories pure and tender
That aye to the heart are dear.

—Isadore Baker
The Northwest Magazine, June, 1890, p. 10.

The Tulip and the Eglantine

The Tulip called to the Eglantine;
"Good neighbor, I hope you see
How the throngs that visit the garden come
To pay their respects to me.

"The florist admires my elegant robe,
And praises its rainbow ray,
Till it seems as if, through his raptured eyes
He was gazing his soul away."

"It may be so," said the Eglantine;
"In a humble nook I dwell,
And what is passing among the great
I cannot know so well.

But they speak of me as the flower of love,
And that low-whispered name
Is dearer to me, and my infant buds,
Than the loudest breath of fame."

—Anonymous
The Rose: Its History, Poetry, Culture and Classification, 1847, pp. 73—74.

June

A sky full of blue and an earth spread with
green,
With fleecy white clouds softly floating
between,
With trees full of leaves and of songsters in
tune,
Oh! what can this be but our beautiful June?

She throws out her signal o'er garden and
wall,
She tosses her banner of roses to all;
No matter what scenes or how sweetly attune,
A month without roses could never be June.

—Sarah E. Howard
Good Housekeeping, June 9, 1888, p. 55.

The Wild Rose

Welcome! Oh, welcome once again,
Thou dearest of all the laughing flowers
That open their odorous bosoms when
The summer birds are in their bowers!
There is none that I love, sweet gem, like
thee,
So mildly through the green leaves stealing;
For I seem, as thy delicate flush I see,
In the dewy haunts of my youth to be;
And a gladsome youthful feeling
Springs to my heart, that not all the glare
Of the blossoming East could awaken there.

Glorious and glad it were, no doubt,
Over the billowy sea to sail,
And to find every spot of the wide world out,
So bright and fair in the minstrel's tale:
To roam by old Tiber's classic tide
At eve, when round the gushing waters
Shades of renown will seem to glide,
And amid the myrtle's flower pride
Walk Italy's soft daughters:
Or to see Spain's haughtier damsels rove
Through the delicious orange grove.

Glorious it were, where the bright heaven
glows,
To wander idly far away,
And to scent the musk'd voluptuous rose
Of beauty, blest Circassia!
To spy some languid Indian maid,
Wooing at noon the precious breeze,
Beneath the proud magnolia's shade;
Or a Chilian girl at random laid
On a couch of amaryllides:
To behold the cocoa-palm, so fair
To the eye of the fair islander.

Glorious Camellian blooms to find,
In the jealous realms of far Japan,
Or the epidendrum's garlands twin'd
Round the tall trees of Hindostan.
All this were glad, and awhile to be
Like a spirit wand'ring gaily;
But oh! What souls, to whome these are free,
Would give them all to share with me
The joys that I gather daily,
When, out in the morning's dewy spring,
I mark the wild Rose blossoming!

When the footpath's winding track is lost
Beneath the deep o'erhanging grass,
And the golden pollen forth is tost
Thickly upon me as I pass;

When England is paradise all over;
When flowers are breathing, birds are singing;
When the honeysuckle I first discover
Balming the air, and in the clover
The early scythe is ringing;
When gales in the billowy grass delight,
And a silvery beauty tracks their flight;

And, more than all, the sweet, wild Rose,
Starring each bush in lanes and glades,
Smiles in each lovelier tint that glows
On the cheeks of England's peerless maids:
Some, with a deeper, fuller hue,
Like lass o'er the foamy milk-pail chanting;
Lighter are some, and gemm'd with dew,
Like ladies whose lovers all are true,
And nought on earth have wanting;
But their eyes on beauteous scenes are bent,
That own them their chief ornament.

But enough —the wild Rose is the queen of
June,
When flowers are abroad and birds in tune.

—Mary Howitt
The Rose: Its History, Poetry, Culture and
Classification, 1847, p. 65.

Love Among the Roses

It was on one Summer's evening,
In the merry month of June
I beheld a dame sitting
'Mid flowers' sweet perfume.
She was a novel reading
Just as I was passing by,
And as she turned another page,
I saw the brightest eye…
A bewitching smile was on her face,
As charming as the poses:
I felt the smart of Cupid's dart:
'Twas love among the roses.

Now, I hate to tell, but then I must;
Within her heart I place my trust;
She was sitting in the garden,
Where the little butterfly reposes;
And how we met, I'll ne'er forget;
'Twas love among the roses.

I passed her house next evening,
The clock had just struck Eight,
And I saw my future happiness:
She was standing by the garden-gate,
She smiled as I approached her,
And I begged her to excuse:

"May I view those pretty flowers?"
She murmured: "If you choose."
I spoke about the violets,
Then finally made proposes:
Thro' the garden we walked, of happiness talked,
'Twas love among the roses.

Now, I hate to tell, but then I must;
Within her heart I place my trust;
She was sitting in the garden,
Where the little butterfly reposes;
And how we met, I'll ne'er forget;
'Twas love among the roses.

I confess I love Matilda:
Matilda, that's her name;
And there is a charm about her,
Which I never can explain.
She dresses up to fashion,
To her style there is no end,
And, of course, she must look dashing;
For, she wears a Grecian Bend.
But she's left her home, and where she's gone
Most everyone supposes;
For, as dear as life is my little wife
'Twas love among the roses.

Now, I hate to tell, but then I must;

Within her heart I place my trust;
She was sitting in the garden,
Where the little butterfly reposes;
And how we met, I'll ne'er forget;
'Twas love among the roses.

—W.H. Delehanty
The New Singer's Journal, 19th-century,
Volume 2, p. 11.

The Immortal Rose

Leafy June grows chill December—
Earth's dull cycle changeth not;
O my love, dost thou remember?
Can it be thou hast forgot?
All the roses seemed to waken:

Now the garden is forsaken,
And the cold wind changeth not.

All the roses woke about us
As we wandered hand in hand;
Sweetest breezes seemed to flout us—
It was June through all the land.
All the flowers so quick to waken
Now are fallen and forsaken,
Save one rosebud in my hand.

Thou didst give me that, and bid me
Keep it close against my heart;
And thy fond endearments chid me
When I knew that we must part.
Thou didst cry, 'While roses waken
Hath the rose thy cheek forsaken?
Rose forget me not, sweetheart!'

I forget thee? I forget thee?

Can the heart forget to live?
Since the day when first I met thee
I remember and forgive.
Love—the love thou didst waken—
Fadeth not, although forsaken;
While life lasteth love shall live.

—Ried, Ellis.
A Crown of Flowers, 1883, pp. 56—57.

The Moss Rose

"I've a call to make," said the rich Moss Rose,
"At the house of a lady fair;
Cousin China Rose, if you'll go with me,
I'll introduce you there.

"'Tis New Year's day; come, do not stay,
But get on your cloak and hood;
You've moped so long by the green-house
fire,
That a walk will do you good."

Then China's Yellow Rose replied,
"You've a terrible climate, dear;
It has made me old before my time,
And bilious too, I fear!

"But I'll put my muff and tippet on,
Since you needs must have me go;
And yet I'm sure I heard a blast,
And saw a flake of snow."

The Moss Rose wrapped her damask robe
Close round her queenly form,
And led her nervous friend along,
Who trembled at the storm.

But the beautiful lady welcomed them
With such a radiant eye,
That they fancied summer had come again,
And winter was quite gone by.

They took their India-rubbers off,
And laid their hoods away,
And whisper'd in each other's ear,
"We should like to spend the day."

She charmed them with her tuneful voice,
Till both were unable to stir;
So there they staid, —and the flowers of love
Have found their home with her.

—L.H. Sigourney.
*The Rose: Its History, Poetry, Culture and
Classification*, 1847, pp. 117—118.

Ballad of Dreamland

I hid my heart in a nest of roses
Far from the glare of midsummer skies,—
There where the humble-bee drowsily dozes,
There where the perfumed breezes rise.
And I said: "As long as the humming-bird
flies
Ceaselessly over thee, O my heart,
From all the lures that the love-god tries,
Forever and ever secure thou art."

And safe it lay as a leaf that reposes
On the river's breast when the twilight dies;
And still it was as a flower that grows is
As a lily that cool in the water lies.
And never a foe came there to surprise
The fortress wherein I hid my heart;
And I said: "Of mortals I am most wise:
Forever and ever secure thou art."

But the queen of the flowers in the garden-
closes,
The maiden with mystical, wonderful eyes,
Whom a wall of scornfulness aye encloses,
Safe from all lover's prayers and sighs—
She for whom never a love may suffice
Out of its fortress drew my heart;

And yet I say on, in braggart-wise,
"Forever and ever secure thou art."

—A.C. Swinburne
The Quest of Heracles and Other Poems,
1893. pp. 44—45.

The Wild Rose

A schoolboy whistling merrily
Upon his homeward way:
A schoolgirl singing cheerily,
So blithely and so gay:
And where two roads cross there they meet;
He casts at her a wild rose sweet;
She laughing runs away,
And nothing does she say.

A youth with lightly moving feet
Advancing mid the throng:
A maiden fair, a maiden sweet,
Who hums an old, old song:
And when they cross their glances meet;
He drops a wild rose at her feet;
She, smiling, moves away,
And nothing does she say.

A manly form waits silently
Within a dim lit hall;
A woman coming quietly
To answer, once for all:
Beneath the crossing arch they meet;
She gives him back a wild rose sweet,
And blushing looks away,—
And nothing does she say.

—I.E.
Good Housekeeping, March, 1889, p. 234.

La Rosière

The pretty custom still lingers in some
villages of France of crowning 'La Rosière.'
A maiden —good, gentle, and modest— is
chosen by the general consent of the villagers,
and crowned with summer flowers as Rosière.

Come, maidens blithe and debonair,
And crown our smiling Rosière.
She must be good, she may be fair,
Whom we would crown as Rosière.
So gentle she —this maiden rare—
That she shall be our Rosière.
And is there heart with sorrow sair?
Sweet solace brings our Rosière.
So true her speech, so pure her air,
We love her for our Rosière.
Our fairest blooms shall wreathe her hair,
And garland her —our Rosière.
So modest she —all unaware
We caught her for our Rosière!
And no reproachful word may dare
Assail our chosen Rosière.
Come, maidens blite and debonair,
And crown our smiling Rosière!
—Clara Thwaites.
A Crown of Flowers, 1883, p. 32.

A Song of the Roses

No beautiful palace have I on the hill,
No pictures to hang in my halls,
But never a painter could match with his skill
The roses abloom on my walls.

Then sing me a song of the rose,
A song that is tender and true!
She wears her red robes like the daintiest
queen,
All gleaming with jewels of dew;

When down my green valley in purple and
gold,
The morning comes dewy and bright,
I look from my window to see them unfold
Their buds at the kiss of the light.

Then sing me a song of the rose,
A song that is tender and true!
She wears her red robes like the daintiest
queen,
All gleaming with jewels of dew!

And when at the ev'ning my labor is o'er,
The shadows grow on the lea,
The breath of the roses floats in at the door,

As if they were talking to me.

Then sing me a song of the rose,
A song that is tender and true!
She wears her red robes like the daintiest
queen,
All gleaming with jewels of dew!

—Anonymous
Home Songster, 1883, p. 69.

The Rose of Stars

When Love, our great Immortal,
Put on mortality,
And down from Eden's portal
Brought this sweet world to be,
At the sublime archangel
He laughed with veilèd eyes,
For he bore within his bosom
The seed of Paradise.

He hid it in his bosom,
And there such warmth it found,
It brake in bud and blossom,
And the rose fell on the ground;
As the green light on the prairie,
As the red light on the sea,
Through fragrant belts of summer
Came this sweet world to be.

And the grave archangel, seeing,
Spread his mighty vans for flight,
But a glow hung round him fleeing
Like the rose of Arctic night;
And sadly moving heavenward
By Venus and by Mars,
He heard the joyful planets
Hail Earth, the Rose of Stars.

—G.E. Woodberry
The Century Magazine, September, 1896, p. 671.

To the Rose

An Ancient Poem Translated

The Spring comes garland bearing,
And wreath and blossom wearing;
And we will aye be singing
The Roses, she is bringing.
Come! Comrades! Songs are ringing
To Summer's Rose! Sweet Summer's Rose.

Like breath from heaven's own portals
Come Roses bright to mortals;
The Graces sow their praises;
The Loves in flow'ry mazes,
Each one, his voice upraises,
To sing with Cithèra's[1] toy.

Plant, pleasing to the Muses,
With love all song infuses;
The fragrance from its treasure
It pours with equal measure
On him, whose touch is pleasure,
Or him who strays in thorny ways.

The wise delight and revel
In Roses' bright apparel;

---

[1] Cithèra: another name for Venus

When purple wine is flowing,
When banquets loud are growing,
The Rose from colours glowing,
Gives crimson leaves for wine-god's wreaths.

The Dawn is rosy-fingered;
O'er nymphs have Rose tints lingered;
Love's colour, blooms yet clearer,
On Rosy-hued Cithèra!
What theme, to poets dearer,
Than soft Rose light on Goddess bright.

This flower takes off diseases,
In sickness gently pleases;
Its old age cannot sever
The scent it loses never;
And dead, we keep forever
The perfumed air of Roses fair.

Come! Hear! Its birth I'm telling:
When Pontus, from his dwelling
Brought forth from Cithèra tender;
The blue seas did surrender
Love's Queen, who rose in splendour
From laughing foam with Gods to roam.

When Zeus his Goddess shewing,
Who, from his brain was growing;
No longer he retained her,

But Queen of War! Proclaimed her;
Athène! Great! He named her;
And forth she came, War-Queen to reign.

Then Earth her bloom unfolded,
And sprays of blossom moulded;
Her glowing Roses forming
With colours from the morning,
Made flowers for Gods adorning—
Thus Earth did bear the Rose Gods wear.

—Anacreontea.
Ancient text; this version translated by Mrs.
Herbert Hills, 1884.

Blossoms

Short Stories About Roses

Three Warnings

I find, my children, that I am growing old, and that it behooves me to write out for your perusal hereafter the history that it is essential you should know, and which, singular as the details may appear under the influence and scepticism of this nineteenth-century, it is still strictly true. I have to relate not only my own personal experience, but that of two of our ancestors.

We have been a family appparently highly favored by fate. You have heard, doubtless, of the talismans possessed by certain noble families, and which were supposed by some mysterious power to bring good-fortune to their owners. Such a one is the famous glass goblet known as the Luck of Eden Hall, and celebrated in verse by Longfellow. We, the Martels, originally of France, but for three generations citizens of the United States, have in our keeping a talisman more potent and more singular in the manifestations of its powers than any other relic of the kind, of which I have ever heard. For it does not simply confer good-luck on its possessors, but it acts the part of a guardian angel.

You know, my children, that our family is a very ancient one. We are supposed to derive our descent from the heroic and intellectual Charles Martel, who governed France so wisely as Mayor of the Palace under the feeblest of the early kings of France. Respecting our claim to consider this great man as our ancestor, I have nothing definite to allege. But this I do know: that the family was an old and honorable one, a race of students, of artists, and of men renowned for their learning and in some cases for their skill as workers in gold and silver and precious stones. Benvenuto Cellini himself was jealous of the talent of Antoine Martel, who was patronized by Diana of Poitiers, and who made for that lady a table-service in gold, wrought with the story of Diana and Endymion, and to whom Queen Claude of France confided the task of mounting her ancestral jewels, the ducal diadem and other crown-jewels of Brittany, into ornaments better fitted for the wife of Francis the First to wear. But it was the father of Antoine, the Martel who flourished in the reign of Louis the Eleventh, who was the true chief of our family. Gilles Martel was a noted physician and was also given to dabbling in astrology and alchemy and other occult sciences. He was in high favor at one time with his keen-witted but superstitious sovereign, and is said to have predicted in a very startling way the tragic fate that some years later befell the reknowned Charles the Bold, Duke of Burgundy. Also, he was much in favor with King Louis's delicate and deformed daughter, the Princess Joan, and did much to alleviate her sufferings during her frequent attacks of illness. During the brief period that she was Queen of France, she made him her court-physician; and when, after her repudiation by her husband, she retired to a cloister, it was by her wish that he still continued his ministrations. I have dwelt thus long on the history of Gilles Martel for a reason that will presently appear.

You are all of you familiar with the subject and aspect of the vast piece of ancient tapestry that has always covered one of the sides of my library-wall, and some amongst you have begged me at times to remove it and to fill the space it occupies with an extra book-case, which is, I confess, much needed. Also, I remember the amazement evinced by you all when, on the occasion of a fire, caused by a defective flue, breaking out in our spare bed-room, I hastened to detach the old tapestry and to bear it out of harm's way before attempting to save anything else, and, in fact, as soon as I had ascertained that your mother and you were out of danger. The fire was extinguished, it is true, without doing any material damage; but you apparently thought that I might have begun by saving our plate and our pictures and also your mother's diamonds. Children, the old tapestry is our Luck of Eden Hall; it is more—it is, as I have said before, our guardian angel.

You remember it, doubtless: the faded group of personages in the foreground, one of whom—a tall, gray-bearded, grave-looking gentleman, wearing a loose black robe and a mortar shaped cap trimmed with fur—is, according to family tradition, the portrait of our ancestor, the learned Doctor Gilles. The other individuals represent certain of the great physician's kinfolk, who had made honorable names for themselves as warriors or as ecclesiastics. But it is only with the figure of Gilles Martel that we have to do, and also with the border of the tapestry, on which is worked at intervals groups of red heraldic roses, each composed of three flowers, these groups being separated by square spaces. In each of these squares is delineated a curious little allegorical picture, the meaning of which has never been explained. The whole piece is in a state of perfect preservation and is a singularly fine specimen of the tapestry-work of the fifteenth century. I need not assure you that it is immensely valuable. But on no consideration, nor at any price that may ever be offered to you, must you be persuaded to part with it. I do not think that you will be willing to contemplate even the possibility of disposing of it, once you have concluded the perusal of this paper.

I must begin my story with the transcription, or rather an abstract, of a document bequeathed by our ancestor, François Martel, who was the grandson of the learned Gilles, and who flourished in the sixteenth century. From his father Antoine, he had inherited great taste and skill as a worker in metals. As a youth, he had embraced the Reformed religion and was a Huguenot of an ardent and pronounced type. This fact did not hinder him from being extensively patronized by the less bigoted of the nobles at the court of Charles IX, though of course he got but few orders from the followers of the Duke de Guise. But, when the bold Protestant hero, Henry of Navarre, came to Paris to wed Marguerite de Valois, the star of the Huguenot goldsmith was in the ascendant. There are extant a number of his drawings of designs for articles of plate and jewelry manufactured by him for the royal pair. Amongst these is a wreath of daisies to be wrought in diamonds, as a gift for the bride, which is altogether exquisite and artistic. But I not think that this charming device was ever reproduced in gold and gems.

Now comes the first strange episode in my strange story. I derive my facts from the parchment record drawn up by François Martel himself, and by him bequeathed to his descendants jointly with the piece of tapestry, which had been left to his father Antoine by Doctor Gilles and which had always been held in high esteem by both father and son, on account of the group of family portraits. The writer declares—I translate from the quaint antique French without attempting, as indeed, it would be vain to do, to reproduce its peculiarities in English—that, one pleasant evening early in June in the year 1572, he was seated alone in his study, having need, he writes, of much meditation concerning the design of the silver ewer ordered from him by Admiral de Coligny. He is especially careful to note that his supper had been of the simplest, consisting of some dried pears and comfits and a single cup of Cyprus wine. He is certain that he had not fallen asleep, as he had been greatly engrossed with his drawings and also much tormented thereby, as he could not work the armorial bearings of the Colignys into his design in a satisfactory manner. Finally, having gotten his sketch into shape, he leaned back in his chair for a few moments' rest and reflection. His eyes naturally fell upon the tapestry which hung upon the wall, and upon which the rays of a full and unclouded summer moon were brightly shining, and especially upon the figure of his grandsire, which was prominent in the foreground. Suddenly it seemed to him as if this figure were slowly rising out of the tapestry; that is to say, it was no longer a flat surface, but was assuming the rounded and prominent contours of a living being or of a graven image. As he gazed, the change became more accentuated and complete, and finally the form took motion as it had assumed shape, and steeped from the hangings to the floor, slowly advancing till it came within a few paces of the table at which the astonished goldsmith sat. He makes special record of the fact that he was not terrified by the apparition, though greatly awed and wonder-stricken.

"My grandson François,": said the form, "I come to warn you, as I shall have the power to warn my descendants hereafter, of a great and impending danger. When you receive from an unknown hand three red roses, be assured that the peril is at hand. Then leave France, with your family and possessions, and without delay. Remember the token—three red roses; and thereafter linger not, but depart at once." Then the room was darkened, as though a cloud had passed over the moon; and, when the light shone out again, the figure had returned to the tapestry, and the room had resumed its wonted aspect.

My ancestor goes on to say that he was deeply impressed with the mysterious warning, and that for some days he thought of little else. Then he became absorbed in the preparations for the wedding of the King of Navarre, and gradually the singular occurrence of that June night faded from his mind. The day of the royal marriage, the 18th of August, at last arrived, and François Martel mingled with the throng at the doors of the Church of Notre Dame, to witness the ceremony, which was performed by the Cardinal de Bourbon and which took place on a lofty stage erected outside of the portal of the catheral. Absorbed as he was in gazing at the bridal party, he was only vaguely conscious of a gentle touch on his right hand;

and, when the marriage was at an end and he
turned away to bend his steps homeward, he
was amazed to find that he was mechanically
holding three red roses that had apparently
been slipped into his hand by some unknown
personage. He looked around and questioned
some of the bystanders as to the giver of the
flowers; but no one had noticed the person
who had left them in Messire Martel's graps,
though several had seen the roses and
remarked upon their beauty.

So greatly was he impressed by this
fulfillment of the phantom's announcement,
that he hastened to put together all his
possessions in the shape of money, jewels,
and and precious metals, not forgetting—as
he specially records—the piece of tapestry,
with other hangings of great price; and he
embarked with all his family at the Louvre
wharf, on a bark hired by himself, for
England, two days after the king's marriage.
He has not failed to record the stupefaction
and indigation of his good wife, Dame
Brigitte, and also of his elder children, at
being thus hurried away on what, in those
days, was a most stupendous journey, and
being forced to lose all the public rejoicings
on the occasion of the royal wedding. Also,
he has set down his own doubts and

misgivings in having undertaken so grave a step as the breaking-up of his home and a flight from his native land, on the word of an apparition and the token of three flowers, that might indeed have come into his possession by accident. But hardly had they arrived in London, nor were the family fully established as yet in a hostelry at Southwark, when the tidings of the bloody massacre of the eve of St. Bartholomew, the 24th of August, reached London. François Martel, as a wealthy and noted Huguenot, would, with all his family, have perished on that night of horrible slaughter, had he disregarded the warning of the phantom and the token of the three roses.

The remainder of the fugitive's history was prosperous and uneventful. He opened a golsdmith's shop at Cheapside, and, as a persecuted Huguenot, his story excited a good deal of sympathy amongst the nobles at the court of Elizabeth. The great queen herself condescended to send for him and to order from him a pomander-chain and some minor matters. Thus patronized by royalty, he flourished exceedingly and was contented and happy in his English home. With this assurance, the document due to his patient pen, and which I have greatly abridged, comes to an end.

The fortunes of the Martel family thereafter have for over two centuries nothing to do with the tapestry portrait of Gilles Martel. After the death of Messire François and the accession to the French throne of Henri IV, his widow and children returned to Paris. In due time, the head of the family married a Catholic lady, and their children were educated in their mother's faith, so that the Martel family was no longer liable to persecution on account of its Protestantism.

In the reign of Louis XIV was founded the banking-house of the Brothers Martel by the two last survivors in the direct line of the descendants of Dr. Gilles. These gentlemen, Jehan and Olivier Martel, founded for the family a new era of prosperity. We, my children, are descended from the first-named, his brother Olivier having died unmarried. During all these years, and despite the journeys and changes of fortune of the family, the piece of tapestry and the narrative of François Martel were always religiously guarded and cared for by the head of the house. Hence the remarkable preservation in which the first-named relic has come down to our day.

I have now come to the epoch of the delivery of the second warning, and I translate from the family papers in my possession, so that such of my descendants that may be unacquainted with the language spoken by their ancestors may read this statement and comprehend the facts as they occurred.

At the accession of Louis XVI to the throne of France, the once numerous race of the Martels had dwindled down to a single survivor, Jules Martel, a prominent and prosperous banker, who had accumulated great wealth, and who had in consequence persuaded the noble family of De Ponteveze to overlook his descent from the Huguenot goldsmith and to bestow one of their demoiselles on him in marriage. Jeanne de Ponteveze was very willing to become Madame Martel, her choice lying between her acceptance of her wealthy suitor and seclusion in a convent. She obtained from the king permission to join her own noble name to that of her husband, and the pair were thereafter known as M. and Mme. Martel de Ponteveze. There was talk of the revival for the husband of one of the dormant titles belonging to the wife's family—a baronry, I believe; but somehow this honor was postponed till titles had become dangerous things in France for their wearers, and the project was dropped. Meantime, the lady had become the close friend and confidante of more than one of the great ladies of the court, the Countess Jules de Polignac and the Princess de Lamballe being of the number. It was said that Madame Martel obliged her aristocratic friends with timely loans of large sums of money through the mediation of her husband, a form of assistance that was peculiarly acceptable in those days of unbounded extravagance of high play at cards. Altogether, the last survivor of the descendants of Gilles Martel had become thoroughly affiliated with the court-party amongst the French aristocracy. His treasured piece of ancestral tapestry decorated the chief drawing-room of his sumptuous hotel in Paris. It was something in his favor, with his new circle of friends, to be able to show that he really possessed ancestors, and one at least, in the person of the learned adviser of Louis XI, of whom he could well be proud. As to the apparition and the warning and the token of the three red roses, as related by the goldsmith François, the astute banker had long before set them down as the figments of an overexcited brain, or as a dream and a series of curious coincidences at the most.

He has not left on record the precise date nor the exact circumstances attending the second appearance of the figure of Gilles

Martel. He states that it was on a moonlit night, and that the form descending from the tapestry addressed him in almost the exact words that François Martel had so carefully written down. Once again was the descendant of the learned doctor warned to flee from France, and once more were three red roses indicated as the token that danger was at hand. And then the figure seemed to retreat backward to the wall, and became again incorporated with the tapestry. Jules Martel was at first less moved by the vision or dream, coupled as it was with the same experience that had befallen his ancestor, than might have been imagined. But he relates in his diary how for some weeks he waited and watched, and in the vague expectation of receiving the token-flowers; but, as time went on without farther incident, he became persuaded that he had fallen asleep on one of the couches in the drawing-room, and had simply dreamed a remarkably vivid dream, colored by his remembrance of the story told by his ancestor.

Time wore on, and the thrilling scenes and dramatic events that preceded the actual outbreak of the great Revolution filled the minds of all men. Jules Martel and his wife, now thoroughly affiliated with the most ultra division of the royalists party, were actors in more than one of the incidents that diversified the prologue to that terrible historical tragedy. And so it chanced that they were present at the banquet given by the officers of the French and Swiss Guards at the theatre of the palace of Versailles. It was a scene never to be forgotten: the fair queen, pale beneath her rouge, the cries and excitement and eager drinking of the healths of the royal party by their military guests, the orchestra pouring forth the melancholy yet impassioned strains of "O Richard, O my king!" the tricolor trampled under foot, the soldiers scaling the boxes to receive from the hands of the ladies the white cockade emblematic of their loyalty; it was a moment whose fervor and enthusiasm might well have persuaded the most lukewarm partisan of royalty that the affections of the nation were really centered on their king and queen. Madam Martel de Ponteveze had just attached one of the rosettes of white ribbon to the shoulder of an ardent young lieutenant, her own nephew, and her husband had smiled his approval of the act, when, on turning from the stage, he saw lying before him, on the ledge of the box, three red roses.

It was rather strange that he took heed at once and practically to the warning of the token-flowers. But Jules Martel was a keen-witted and sensible man, and was not wholly blinded by his prejudices in favor of the aristocratic set in which he had gained a precarious footing by his marriage. He was in reality a roturier[2], and he knew it, and he had doubtless often meditated with many misgivings over the coming tempest, whose dark clouds and muttering thunder could be ignored by no such intelligent observer as himself, and especially one whose senses were not blunted by the prejudices of race. His own convictions lent weight to the warnings of the phantom and the flowers. He hastened to transfer to England his family and such of his possessions as could be taken thither. His banking-house was left in the charge of one of his junior partners, and, long before the full horror of the Reign of Terror had burst upon his native land, he was established, with his family, in a pleasant quarter of London. There he and his wife came to be considered as a very providence for the exiled French nobles. Many of the kinsfolk of Madame Martel—and among them the young Lieutenant de Ponteveze, who had figured at the banquet at Versailles—

---

[2] roturier: commoner

perished by the guillotine, a fate that would doubtless have befallen both Jules Martel and his wife, had not that strange vision interposed to save them.

Such, my children, was the experience of my great-great-grandfather. It was I myself who was to be the next of the descendants of Gilles Martel to receive the spectral warning.

Early in the present century, the sole representative of the Martel family was a brave colonel who had achieved distinction in the army during the triumphant campaigns of the great Napoleon. After the overthrow of the hero and the restoration of the Bourbons, Colonel Martel, disgusted with matters and things in his native land, decided upon taking up his residence in a foreign country. He had several friends and more than one relative residing in Louisiana, and he fixed upon that young and thriving Republic of the United States as his future home. Indeed, it was said to be Lafayette himself whose counsels had guided him in the selection of his new place of abode. The colonel purchased a plantation on the banks of the Mississippi, not far from New Orleans, and settled down to his new mode of life with more readiness than one would have imagined from his military antecedents. His son and only child Louis—

your grandfather, my children, was a typical Southern planter, kind-hearted and amiable, with courteous though languid manners, and sufficiently free from sectional prejudices to send me to be educated at Harvard College. There I imbibed a certain distaste for plantation-life which stood me in good stead at a momentous crisis in my life, by swaying my decision in favor of the line of action which I subsequently adopted.

My father was barely past middle age when he died very suddenly of an attack of yellow fever, that malady being then raging in an epidemic form in our State and carrying off the hardiest and best-seasoned of our citizens. It was only after his death, and on looking through his papers, that I became acquainted with the narratives of François and of Jules Martel, and of the importance to our family of the ancestral piece of tapestry. It is true that my father had frequently referred to the tapestry itself as a precious family relic, and had promised more than once to tell me the legend connected with it; but, with his usual indolence and fondness for procrastination, he had put off doing so till death overtook him and sealed his lips forever. It took me some time to decipher the quaint old French of the document drawn up by François Martel, and, though I was much interested in it, and also in the meager notes left by the banker Jules, I must say that I was not particularly impressed by the family apparition and the two warnings. Viewed by the light of the skepticism of the nineteenth-century, the two adventures appeared to me but curious coincidences resulting from the unconsciously formed convictions of the two intelligent men respecting the current of public events in their day, which convictions had shaped their dreams and had caused them to look upon a casual gift of flowers as a mysterious and supernatural occurrence.

Only the eldest of you can even faintly remember the agitation and excitement caused in the South, in the spring and summer of 1860, by the approaching election of Mr. Lincoln. We spent the months of July, August, and September, as was our wont, at the Northern watering-places, returning home in the first days of October. My mind was very full of the crisis which I saw was approaching, and which I feared was inevitable. Perhaps it was this current of thought which shaped the incident which I am now about to relate.

Late one evening, soon after our return to our plantation, I was seated alone in my library, engaged in writing letters. Your mother had sent all the children off to bed some hours before, and had herself gone upstairs. I was writing at an office-table placed in the centre of the room, the only light in the apartment being that of a shaded student's-lamp, all of whose rays were concentrated on a circumscribed spot on the table. On the wall opposite me, and consequently wholly in shadow, hung the antique tapestry, its faded hues showing indistinct and formless. I had finished one of the series of letters on which I was engaged, and was looking around in quest of an envelope, when my eye was attracted by a faint light quivering over the surface of the tapestry. At first, it was not vivid, resembling in its character the bluish luminous vapors of phosphorous; but it gradually became steadier and brighter as I gazed, 'til finally by its luster I discerned the figure of Gilles Martel, wholly detached from the tapestry and standing—as it seemed—within a few paces of the table at which I sat. Then I became aware, not exactly by hearing the words, but as though their meaning were conveyed to my brain without the intervention of any of my senses, of the following communication: "Son of my sons, you and your family are threatened with danger and disaster. When, like two of your ancestors, you receive the token of the three red roses, then hasten to depart, for great calamities are about to befall the land. Seek peace and prosperity in a distant country. Remember and heed my warning. Farewell." Then the pale light faded away into darkness, and I saw nothing more. I caught up my lamp and removed the shade, throwing its rays full upon the tapestry. The faded figures of Gilles Martel and his kinsfolk were all in their places, unchanged and motionless.

Some weeks later came election day.

I drove in to New Orleans to be on hand to receive the latest tidings. It was late in the evening when, having learned the final and decisive results in favor of the Republican candidate, I went, with a heavy heart, in search of my carriage. As I sprang into the vehicle, my attention was attracted by an object lying on the front seat and dimly visible by the light of the carriage-lamps. I took it up to examine it. It was a cluster composed of three red roses growing on one stem.

"Caesar," I called to the coachman, "who put these flowers in the carriage?"

"Flowers, sir? Dunno, sir. I've seen nobody hereabouts, sure."

Children, my story is at an end. Acting on my own convictions no less than in obedience to the spectral warning, I hastened to dispose of my Southern property and took my departure for Paris. Once again I enjoin on you the necessity of the careful preservation of that invaluable relic. And, if ever again the message of Gilles Martel and the token of the three roses be united to tell of a coming disaster and to counsel instant flight, take example by the action of François and Jules Martel and of myself, and at once obey the warning.

—Lucy B. Hooper
Peterson's Magazine, 1890, pp. 347—352.

A Rose for To-Day

"Tell me a story, please," said little
Robbie, the only child of the pretty gentle-
faced widow who was staying at the East
Shore Hotel, a well-known resort on Long
Island Sound.

"Once upon a time—" Maud began.

"The stage is coming down the Point!"
Cried one of the girls, from a hammock.

"Once upon a time," Maud repeated, "a
princess sat looking out over the water,
wishing—"

"I don't like that story," interrupted
Robbie. "Mamma told it to me, this
afternoon; and the prince never came back,
although she wished it ever so long."

"But the prince of my story did, my
boy," laughed Maud.

"Here is the stage," said Major West,
Maud's devoted admirer. And, as he spoke,
the solitary passenger alighted —a dark man,
apparently in feeble health: for he came up the
piazza steps leaning on the arm of a body
servant and went immediately to the room for
which, it seems, he had telegraphed.

"The prince has come, Robbie,"
whispered Maud. But she stopped suddenly

at the sight of the white face of the boy's mother. What could it mean? Was there any connection, she wondered, between this newcomer and Margaret Vane's sorrow?

Whether this was so or not, from that day a change came over the shy silent widow. Before this, she had always pleaded some excuse for not joining our sailing parties, picnics and other excursions; but now she was the first to propose them and the last to suggest returning.

One day, when we came back, the sick stranger was seen for the first time on the piazza. He was occupying Mrs. Vane's low rocker, in a shady corner.

"Someone ought to take care of the poor fellow," said Maud to Mrs. Vane. "The night air is coming on, and he is sound asleep; it is dangerous, especially as his cough is so bad."

When the stranger woke from his sleep, half an hour after, he was surprised to find a gay-striped afghan, soft and warm, and exhaling a faint rose perfume, thrown over him.

"I will not trouble you long —not long," he murmured, as if still half unconscious. And he rose and moved feebly away.

The next morning broke cold and rainy, with a high wind. All day, the invalid occupied a seat near the fire which had been kindled in the public sitting-room. He spoke but little. Often, his eyes wandered to little Robbie, who played about; and, once or twice, they furtively sought Mrs. Vane. When evening came, Margaret was asked to sing, for all knew how fine her voice was. She sat down and began to play. At first, the notes throbbed with the sound of victory after a long and wearisome march; then a waltz, softly, dreamily played, followed; and one had only to close one's eyes to see a lighted room and the figures swaying in rhythmic time with the music.

"Mamma, please sing your pretty song," Robbie called. "The Rose Song."

The sick guest stirred uneasily in his chair by the fire.

Mrs. Vane hesitated for a moment, then played the prelude, tender and low and sorrowfully sweet, and afterward sang, in her wonderful way, these quaint words:

What flower shall I wear, my love to show?
A lily pale —a lily? Ah, no!
For yesterday's dead, when lilies did blow.

A pansy sweet —a pansy? Ah, no!
For summer will come and summer will go,
And pansies will blossom beneath the snow.

A flow'r for today, my love to show—
A deep-red rose, that brightly will glow
And will tell my love that I love him so.

During the singing, the face of the stranger wore an expression of utter weariness. The eyes were closed. "Can it be," Maud thought. "That the end is so near? Major West says so. Perhaps tomorrow, the windows will be darkened, and we who laugh tonight will tread softly and talk in whispers of the dead man."

When Margaret Vane arose from the piano, she too saw the white face, with the strange look upon it. A great tear, at that moment, dropped from the closed eyelids and fell upon the thin hand.

She crossed the room with a hurried step and knelt by the invalid's side.

"Robert!" She cried. "Robert! My husband!" Oh, the pathos of that cry! "You are dying, and have no word for me! Yet you have tears for our little song!"

He opened his eyes and looked at her eagerly.

"Not tears for the song, Margaret, but for the cruel years that have slipped between," he said, "and have taken from me my wife and child."

"Oh, Robert! Robert!" She exclaimed, in a voice in which incredulity and tenderness mingled with a pathos which no words could describe.

"No man ever more highly prized his treasures than I did mine," he went quickly on, answering the passionate appeal in her tone. "How could you distrust me? Oh, Margaret! Margaret! How was it possible that, even for a moment, you could doubt my love?"

"Robert, what was I to think —how could I help doubting?" She cried, with a rush of hot tears. "Oh, forgive me if I have wronged you —forgive me!"

"You wronged your own heart as sorely as mine," he answered, laying his hand softly on her bowed head. "I see that now —now when it is too late."

"No! No!" She groaned. "It is not too late —it shall not be!"

"Hush!" He said, with a slow painful smile. "It is not for you or me to decide or rebel against; whatever the burden, our duty is plain —to bear it as patiently as we can."

"It is too hard —too hard!" She sighed.

"Nothing is too hard when the sorrow is not of our own causing," he replied.

"But this is my work, you say," she cried. "Oh, if I had been more patient —if I had only waited —only waited!"

"Yes; you might have trusted me."

"I had —I had —until —until—"

Her voice broke; her eyes were raised to his face for an instant; then her head sank again on the arm of the chair.

"You would have only had to wait a day longer," he said, in a repressed difficult voice.

"A day? Only one day?"

"Only that, Margaret —only that."

"Oh, this is too terrible!" She exclaimed. "And I cannot understand —I cannot!"

"When I reached home, you were gone," the husband continued, in the same choked difficult tone. "Now Robbie has completely forgotten me —completely; and you—"

"They told me you were not coming — and I thought they knew!" She interrupted.

"They?" He repeated, with a sudden thrill of passion in his tone.

"Yes —your own relatives!"

"Only one of my relatives, I think, Margaret," was the rather cold response.

"Oh, Robert —my husband!" She cried again, with passionate yearning and regret. "I only began to think there might be a mistake when your cousin sent for me, in her last illness."

"She made no confession?"

"She could not talk connectedly; the few broken explanations she attempted were so vague that I could not catch them; and— and—"

"Well, Margaret, well?"

"Oh, I suppose my terrible pride stood in the way," she sobbed. "I could not be sure that I had been mistaken. I could not go back without one word from you —I might have found my presence unwelcome. I did think of trying —I did!— But that fear restrained me, held me fast. Oh, I knew that to see you and find I was not wanted would drive me mad."

He lifted her head with his frail hand and looked into her face, while a smile of heavenly sweetness illumined his own.

"Margaret, I love you now, and I loved you then."

What did it all mean? She was not a widow, then; but had parted from her husband, and in anger.

We all rose, as by one impulse, and left the room; left them together, husband and wife and child.

Afterward, when the happy reconciliation was complete, we who had learned to know and love Margaret Vane heard the whole story of the misunderstanding which had resulted in such long years of separation and misery to the pair who had loved each other devotedly in spite of their foolish pride and hastiness.

Mrs. Vane sent for Maud, to whom she had always felt most closely drawn, and, with trembling lips and eyes in which joy and peace shone through tears, told the tenderly sympathizing girl the whole sorrowful story.

"We were very young, both of us, and I— I behaved like a silly child; but I have been bitterly punished for my folly —surely it was nothing more. I meant to do right," said Margaret.

"I am sure you did," Maud answered, consolingly. "And now all is well —never mind the unhappy past."

"Ah! But it is difficult to forget, and besides I must explain. Robert was not to blame —it was my fault and —his cousin's."

Maud gently pressed the speaker's hand as she paused an instant, almost overcome.

"You see," went on Margaret, "she had loved him, poor thing, all her life. She was terribly angry when he married me, but she did not allow me to see that. I trusted and loved her. Robert went away unexpectedly — it was not his own affair, but somebody else's trouble —a friend's."

Mrs. Vane stopped a moment, almost overcome by the thought of her cruel misjudgement, while Maud whispered:

"Do not tell me. I know it is all right."

The other shook her head and continued:

"He was detained longer than he expected to be. His cousin told me he was never coming back —that — that he had left me forever —gone." Her voice broke. "— With someone whom he loved better. I could not bear it, so I took Robbie and went away in my anger. I had enough to live on, and, when Robert came back, he believed what his cousin told him of me. Ah! It was too dreadful!"

"He will live now," Major West said to Maud, as they separated for the night.

Again the morning dawned, but now a sunny sky was overhead. We were awaiting the arrival of the stage, in which Maud was to leave.

"I knew you understood," Margaret was saying to her, "The night you told me Robert would never get well if not better cared for."

"And I was quite sure that I was indeed cared for," her husband broke in, with a smile, lifting a corner of the afghan which was folded across his lap.

"We are to have a cottage of our own here, next summer, and you must come and visit us then." And, looking into wee Robbie's pleading brown eyes, what could Maud answer but "Yes"?

Major West now approached, holding a crimson rose, which he held out to Maud.

"Lilies for yesterday, pansies for tomorrow, but roses for today," he said. "Will you wear it for me, Maud?"

And, for answer, she fastened it in her shining braids of hair, and smiled back at him as he escorted her to the stage.

—Clara E. Samuels
Peterson's Magazine, December, 1889, pp. 82—84.

Among the Roses

Madge Vernon made as pretty a picture, in her Gainsesborough hat and Marie Antoinette fichu, as ever Sir Joshua Reynolds himself painted. Madge was one of the few girls who could venture to dress picturesquely, and she knew it; and with her keen, artistic feeling, she hit the mark invariably; for though always original and effective, she was never conspicuous, or loud. Today she was out in the garden, gathering roses to adorn the parlors, intending, however, to select a few of the choicest for her hair, for she was going to a dinner-party in an hour or two at Mrs. Lyttimer's. But it was late in the season, and the finest of the roses were gone. She found plenty that were good enough for her vases, but none that were sufficiently beautiful for her hair. "Dear me," she said, "what shall I do? I had set my heart on natural flowers for tonight; and there isn't one here that's fit to wear."

Just at that instant, looking through the garden-gate, she saw an old woman with a basket on her arm, passing down the village street. "Oh! There's Mrs. Crowe," she cried, "the very person I want." Mrs. Crowe was a vendor of flowers, well known to the neighborhood, who always had the choicest hot-house roses, "real Boston beauties," as she boasted to her customers. In a moment Madge had darted through the gate, and stood at her side. So sudden was the appearance of the young girl, however, that a vicious looking dog, a mirror of ugliness, which was trotting at Mrs. Crowe's side, led by a cord, began to bark viciously at our heroine, struggling to spring at her, and making as grand an uproar as if he had a little apparatus for producing thunder inside his horrid, dwarfed body.

"Law me, Miss Madge, if it ain't you!" Exclaimed the elderly dame, apparently as much astonished to see the young lady at the entrance of her own domain as if she had encountered her at the top of Mount Ararat. "Well, I never did! Blowsey, you bad dog, if you don't stop barking, I don't know what I won't do to you!"

"Oh, Mrs. Crowe," cried Madge. "Haven't you some flowers for me?"

"Lord bless your innocent soul, hain't I jist!" Responded Mrs. Crowe. "Roses, buds and full-blown, my dear, that would outdo any of Solomon's, or Absolom's, or any of the rest of 'em in Shiray or Sheba. There's wi'lets, too, and crocuses and sich, for there's doins at the Temperance Hotel tonight, and they engaged me to bring 'em; but law, Miss Madge, you may flower a supper-table, till it's worse than the desert a bustin' into rose, as the Scripture says; you can't make the men see how pretty it is, as well I ought to know, after all the trouble I've had in my day, a raisin' five on 'em, not to mention Crowe himself and his old pa, which was a deal wearinger than the whole caboodle put together, and him on crutches at that."

By this time, she had set the basket on the ground, and taken off the paper laid over the top, though sorely impeded in her movements by the leaps and springs of Blowsey, who barked incessantly.

"What lovely rose-buds," cried Madge, "the very things I wanted."

"And have 'em you shall," said Mrs. Crowe, "if all the Temperance folks in the town should get angry."

Here Mrs. Crowe was interrupted by Blowsey's artfully twitching the cord from her hand, and disappearing round the corner. The old woman shouted after him in vain, and to add to her distress, the barks and yelps of sundry dogs rose high in the air, and it was apparent that a battle was being waged.

"He'll be killed —he'll be killed —the ungrateful little beast!" Moaned Blowsey's owner. "And he knows that my eyesight's so bad I really need him to get along!"

"I'll watch your basket for you while you go after him," Madge said kindly; and Mrs. Crowe set off round the corner, in her turn, alternately coaxing and execrating the wicked Blowsey, as she fled.

There Madge stood, guarding the basket, with a bunch of her own roses in her hand, as if she were a flower-girl, holding out her fragrant wares for sale to any chance passer-by. Nearly opposite where she was standing, a street debouched into the broad road, and a gentleman, coming up that street, caught sight of the pretty figure, and stared with all his might: for, though he was a man who had wandered in many climes, and thought himself, as sated travelers are apt to do, worlds beyond the reach of a new experience or surprise, this graceful, elegant creature, certainly was a revelation in the way of a flower-seller, such as neither Florence or Naples had ever shown him. Before he could recover sufficiently from his astonishment to decide what could be the meaning of the tableau, round the corner opposite that down which Mrs. Crowe had disappeared a trio of drunken fellows approached from the direction of one of the factories.

"H'here's a go!" Cried one. "I s-say, my girl, give us a kiss, and we'll buy your whole basket."

Before Madge had even time to know that she was frightened, the gentleman who had been watching her dashed across the road, treated the speaker to a blow, which sent him sprawling in the dust, and with his other arm knocked the second man backward, though the wall saved him from a tumble.

"Just step inside the gate," he said to Madge; and Madge obeyed mechanically, snatching up the basket as she fled.

But there was to be no battle. The man who had been knocked down got up swearing. But his companions pulled him hastily away, either sufficiently sober to be able to recognize that he had received his just deserts, or else too wise to attempt a struggle with so powerful and skilful an antagonist as the strange gentleman. Madge, looking through the gate, thought this new Perseus handsome enough, and big enough, to have served as a model for Hercules in the full maturity of manhood.

"Be off, you two there," he said. "You are sober enough to know what you are about —and take that rascal with you."

The ruffians evidently considered his advice worth following, and slunk round the corner as rapidly as their unsteady legs would carry them.

At the same instant, up rushed Mrs. Crowe, dragging Blowsey, he barking wildly, and she so completely out of breath that she could hardly gasp: "Oh, Miss Madge —I beg pardon— to think of leaving you —a basket— this disgraceful beast— oh!"

Madge got her wits back.

"It is no matter, Mrs. Crowe," she said. "See, I have taken several rose-buds —come to the house tomorrow." Then she turned to the gentleman and added, "I owe you a great many thanks," and her lips began to tremble, as she realized from what annoyance he had saved her.

The handsome Hercules, or Perseus — which shall we call him?— only lifted his hat, and bowed, and Madge rushed away up to the house, just stopping on the verandah long enough to cast back one glance. Hercules was still standing at the gate with Mrs. Crowe, and her basket before him, and Blowsey frisking aimlessly about his legs.

Miss Evans, and her niece Madge, were somewhat late in entering Mrs. Lyttimer's drawing-room. The rest of the company were already assembled, and were all known to Madge except one, a stranger, and that stranger her Hercules.

"Miss Evans, you have heard me talk of my nephew, Hugh Greatorex," said Mrs. Lyttimer, "and here he is." Then, turning to Madge, she said: "Hugh —Mr. Greatorex— Miss Vernon."

Madge saw that he wore, in the button-hole of his coat, a tiny rose-bud, an own sister to that which decorated her hair. Dinner was now announced. It devolved upon Mr. Greatorex to lead her in, and somehow, the roses, and the little secret shared between them, seemed to make them old acquaintances at once.

But Aunt Jane watched their animated conversation with angry eyes. She had never seen Hugh Greatorex before, but she had heard of him; and heard of him as one of the worst men that ever lived. Mrs. Lyttimer knew it; had often groaned when she talked of him; and now, here he was, a guest under her roof, sitting by Madge at table, and talking as easily as if he had not a mountain-load of

unrepented sins on his soul; laughing, too —
actually laughing. Aunt Jane shuddered.

She would have it out with Laura
Lyttimer, she said to herself, before she left
the house —that she was determined on! But
she broke her vow. For after dinner, Hugh
Greatorex came up, and began talking to her,
and he was so pleasant that she forgot all her
resolve —forgot who he was, and his
wickedness, until she had asked him to come
over to The Nest, and had been so cordial and
friendly that to retreat from the position
would be difficult.

He came the very next day. Back of
Miss Jane's old house there were pleasant
shrubberies, the flower-garden being in front;
and back of the shrubberies was a steep hill;
and as Miss Jane and her niece were walking
in the shrubberies, down plunged Hercules.

"I did not dream that I was entering
your domain pell-mell," said he, after making
his salutations. "I meant to call— you said I
might, Miss Evans— but I went out for a
stroll —lost my way— tumbled down the hill
and here I am."

He laughed so pleasantly that Miss Jane
laughed, too. More than that, the usually
inflexible old woman forgot the vows she had
formed during the night, and talked a long

while with the young man before she
recollected his wickedness and the necessity
for guarding Madge against his machinations.
She had not yet told her niece all the dreadful
stories connected with Hugh Greatorex's
name —she meant to— but during this visit,
he made himself so charming again that she
began to wonder if he could be so black as he
was painted; and determined to put off
exposing him, and his sins, until she had seen
Mrs. Lyttimer.

But Mrs. Lyttimer had caught cold the
evening of her dinner, and had now an attack
of lumbago; and was so miserable for a
fortnight, that she would not see even her
friend, Miss Evans; and when that fortnight
ended, Hugh Greatorex had become an almost
daily visitor at The Nest. Aunt Jane liked him
immensely, and had never told Madge a word
of his history, for she had now decided that it
would not be necessary. She had received a
letter from Morton Walsh, a distant relative.
Morton was coming back from the South; had
determined to propose to Madge, and had
written to Aunt Jane, asking her to keep his
secret. Now a union between the pair was
what Miss Evans had always intended. She
had only been vexed at Morton's negligence.
That Madge could refuse never entered her

head any more than I presume it did Mr. Walsh's, who was accustomed to having Miss Jane and his pretty cousin do whatever he wished, and had always meant to marry Madge, whenever it should be his lordly will and pleasure.

As soon as Mrs. Lyttimer was better, she decided to leave home for a few weeks, in order to consult some pet physician in New York. Aunt Jane went twice to see her, but on both occasions other visitors were present and no conversation of a private nature could take place.

Hugh Greatorex accompanied his aunt, so Miss Evans concluded that the matter had arranged itself. He was gone, and Morton would soon arrive. She was certain Madge had appeared quite excited over the idea of Morton's visit. No doubt, she had loved him all her life: and Aunt Jane heaved a sigh of content to think that her imprudence in so freely admitting Greatorex had done no harm. Madge had not even seemed to think twice about his going away. But he was charming, in spite of his wickedness, thought Aunt Jane, and often she caught herself wishing that her model Morton were half so pleasant; and she wondered, as life has often forced many of us to do, why virtue should so frequently be stiff and priggish, and vice sometimes wear a front so enticing.

But Aunt Jane's comfortable state of mind was suddenly disturbed, for only three days after Hugh Greatorex's departure, he appeared at The Nest again; and any surprise at his coming was confined to the spinster, for Madge did not show the slightest.

"I did not dream of seeing you," said Aunt Jane.

"Oh, I only went to take care of my aunt," he replied, "and returned at once, for she wanted me to be in the house, while she was gone. She is remodeling a portion of the old wing, you know, and was afraid the workmen would make mistakes, if I did not promise to superintend them."

"Much you must know about it!" Quoth the spinster, giving vent to her vexations in this way.

"I ought," he said, smiling, "I once studied under an architect, expecting to adopt his profession."

"And why didn't you?" Aunt Jane asked, a little irritably, thinking that if he had done so, he would be out of the way now.

"Because an old uncle, good naturedly, left me so much money that I was able to follow my own devices," he said.

"People's devices are very often only Satan's, in disguise," cried Aunt Jane, and felt herself growing so cross that she decided it would be better bred to leave the room, at least till she had recovered her equanimity.

She went off to the garden and the fresh air put her in such good humor that she was able to again to remember Morton's intention, of at last claiming Madge, and that, therefore, Hugh Greatorex's return was a matter of no consequence.

But she felt now that she must tell Madge something of the reports, since Hugh was to remain an indefinite length of time in the neighborhood. Morton might be displeased. Morton was very particular, and so dreadfully good himself, that he was apt to be very severe upon the weaknesses of frailer mortals.

Yet, an hour after Aunt Jane had formed these wise resolves, she, with an inconsistency which was delightful, positively asked Hugh Greatorex to come back to dinner that night, and never remembered till it was too late, that she ought not to have done so. Some tiresome visitors having come in, and absorbed Madge's attention, Hugh went off into the garden, and joined Miss Jane, and talked her leagues away from the recollection of her prejudices, in less than fifteen minutes. And in taking leave, he had said, "It is so stupid taking one's dinner alone in that great room."

On which she had answered, impulsively, "Then come and eat it here —we are not stupid— seven, sharp," and the young fellow was so grateful, and said so many amusing things, that it was not until he had gone, and she was on her way into the drawing-room, to be civil to Madge's guests, that she had leisure to repent, and to promise her conscience never so to err again.

But it would do no harm, she said to herself, Morton would soon arrive. And so Miss Jane consoled herself, only, she must caution Madge, she added.

But fate sent the spinster to bed that very night, for a week, with a vile neuralgic attack; and she could think of nothing, save her aches and pains. Madge was the most delightful, patient nurse in the world; but Aunt Jane, with all her little faults, was not selfish, and took care that the girl should spare time, each day, from her duties to have a long walk or ride.

Sometimes Madge mentioned having met Hugh Greatorex; but latterly, she seldom did that; and Aunt Jane concluded that he was very busy about the alterations in Mrs. Lyttimer's house, and considered Madge's slight mention of him a good sign —only, of course, no good sign was needed. Morton had written that he meant to propose to Madge, and there could be no doubt of her answer; she had always done what Morton bade her. Aunt Jane had brought her up for Morton's future wife, and, naturally, she would only find her greatest happiness in accepting the decrees.

Altogether, by the time Aunt Jane began to consider herself quite reestablished in health, these young people had known each other exactly a month, and my wise philosophers, say what you like, there are seasons in this existence, as we less sternly practical people well know, when a month counts for a great deal. Four whole weeks, and nearly half a one over —thirty-one complete days! Ah! Yes, it is possible to live as much in that length of time —real life— as could be spread over the space of years, and yet leave the years comfortably filled— philosophy and common sense to the contrary notwithstanding.

Hugh Greatorex was very kind and attentive to Miss Jane, when she was able again to go downstairs. He ransacked all the florists' hot houses within leagues for flowers. He quite made the fortune of Mrs. Crowe; he sent to New York for delicious tropical fruits; he came daily to drive her out, refusing to believe that she could be safe under the guardianship of any other Jehu. He showed himself in every way so delightful, that more than once, Aunt Jane was horrified to find her vagrant fancy wishing that Morton could acquire something of his manners, then rejoiced to think that Madge was so much wiser than her elderly self, and perfectly content with Morton, and his doings and sayings.

Aunt Jane was not given to confidences; certainly, if she had felt in need of a confident, when her plans for Madge and Morton were concerned, she would not have chosen Hugh Greatorex. Yet she told him the secret, though she did not realize that she had so done. It came about in this way. Hugh had taken her for a drive, and as the carriage turned into the highroad, they met the postman going up to the house.

"Any letters for me?" Called Aunt Jane, and the conscientious postman handed her two.

Hugh insisted on her reading her epistles. The last she opened was from

Morton. He might be expected, he wrote, in the course of a week, and he talked, too, so freely of his intentions in regard to Madge — evidently considering the affair as completely settled as the old maid herself— that the spinster had her head and heart so full of the matter, that she began talking to Hugh, and as I said, without knowing what she was doing, had revealed the secret, only with a variation from the exact truth which was perfectly unintentional, for Aunt Jane would rather have gone to the stake than prevaricate; but her way of relating the matter gave the impression to her listener, that Madge and the model Morton were positively engaged.

A very quiet listener Hugh proved, and this encouraged Aunt Jane to enlarge upon her theme. If she had looked at him, she might have been startled to see how pale he had grown; how hard and firm his mouth was set, under the curves of his moustache, and how strangely dead and cold his eyes stared straight before him; but she did not look. We seldom notice other people, when we are full of ourselves, or our plans —and that is almost always.

"But, bless me!" Cried the old maid, at last. "I am talking riddles, and you must be wishing me in Jericho."

She laughed, as if it were the best joke in the world, and Hugh laughed, too. If the exigencies of this hard old world ever forced you to laugh, when the sound of your own merriment cut your heart like a two-edged sword, you may understand how Hugh Greatorex felt.

They talked of other things. Aunt Jane had a charming drive, for Hugh was uncommonly amusing, and she was sorry when it ended. Hugh refused to go into the house; excused himself when she invited him to come back, and share their dinner; but Aunt Jane was occupied with Morton's coming, and thought little of the young man's refusal, and nothing of his manner; and, indeed, was unconscious that she had given him more than the vaguest hint of how matters stood in her family.

Hugh Greatorex did come to the house the next day, however. But Miss Jane was out. So Hugh Greatorex found Madge alone, in the pretty, old fashioned morning room; and Madge, more observant of his every mood than she was conscious, perceived, the moment he entered, a great, inexplicable change in his demeanor.

Now, though this pair had quickly drifted into a pleasant intimacy, I must do them the justice to say that there had not been the slightest approach to flirtation, or love-passages of any sort, as yet. Madge was not a flirt, and as for loving the man, or being loved by him, I dare say that the bare idea would have appeared unmaidenly to her, considering how brief had been the term of their acquaintance, though it did not seem brief to Madge, all the same. She had grown so rapidly accustomed to his friendship, that it appeared as natural a possession as if she had owned it all her life.

But, this morning, there was a change in him —he was cold, constrained; began a topic, and left it, abruptly; twice answered her almost fretfully, then apologized; and finally, out came the truth.

"I believe I am cross," he said.

"I am quite certain of it," returned Madge, laughing. "Not exactly that, either, but out of spirits."

"And no wonder," said he; "I am going away."

"Going away!" She repeated, not well knowing what she said.

"Yes; I leave for New York this evening."

"Indeed!" Said she, having found time to be puzzled by a strange flutter at her heart

—a little vexed, too, but whether with him for going away, or herself for caring, she could not have told. "I wish you a pleasant journey, I am sure."

"And that is all?" Cried he.

"Well, I think that is the most appropriate wish I could make," she answered, laughing again, though not so easily as before.

"I suppose it is," said he, with a gloom as deep as Hamlet's.

"Your journey is rather sudden, is it not?" She asked, just because silence was so intolerable, that she must say something. "I suppose you are tired of this dull place —and no wonder— I quite envy you going where you please."

"I am not tired, and heaven knows nobody need envy me!" He cried, roused to a pitch of desperation by her words, which, in his general feeling of ill-usage, sounded downright cruel. "I never dreamed, until yesterday, of going —but I shall— I must— I have nothing to stay for."

"Oh!" Gasped Madge, so bewildered, between surprise at his conduct and this inexplicable pain, which seemed to take her breath, that she could not articulate another syllable.

"I am going," he repeated. "I— I don't expect you to miss me; you will not have time."

"One has always time to miss one's friends," Madge said, his confusion somehow giving her a little confidence, though his words hurt her so, that she could not resist adding, "You ought not to say such things; it is very unkind."

"I did not mean to be— I— I beg your pardon!" He fairly groaned. "I— I'm making a fool of myself— but you see it was so sudden. I have just been living in a dream, and now I am awake, and— and this is all I have left!"

And out of his pocket he pulled an envelope; opened it, and showed her a glimpse of a withered rose.

"Oh!" Gasped Madge again, and in a second wished that her guardian angel had had the presence of mind to choke her, before she could utter the ejaculation. But she was a sensible young woman, and hated mysteries, and she got her courage back, and said, bravely, "I don't understand you in the least, and— and I wish you would explain." There was such pain and anguish in his face and eyes, that she could only remember he suffered— though why, she could not tell.

"Explain?" Repeated he. "There's no need to explain! I— I have been a fool— I told you so— and you are engaged to your cousin Morton; so there's nothing for it but to go away, and I am going. Of course, I could not expect you to tell me; there's nobody to blame but myself."

"Who told you I was engaged to my cousin Morton?" Broke in Madge, so outraged by the idea that she forgot everything else.

"Well— perhaps nobody in so many words— but— but I quite understand! I'm very impertinent— I beg your pardon! You see I've been a fool, and when I knew from what your Aunt Jane said—"

"Hey-day, who is taking my name in vain?" Cried the spinster, appearing in the open doorway, just in time to catch his last words. "Are you abusing me behind my back, Hugh Greatorex? I shall write to Laura Lyttimer at once, and—"

Aunt Jane had returned from her walk, in excellent spirits. But, as she approached near enough to see the faces and attitudes of the young people, she stopped, and her sentence died in a gurgle.

There Hugh stood, grasping the envelope that contained the treasured flower.

There stood Madge, regarding Aunt Jane, like a young Nemesis, with something so appalling in her wrathful glance, that if the spinster had had leisure to think of mythology, she would have compared her to Medusa, at least.

"Aunt Jane," cried Madge, in her clear, youthful voice, "come in and shut the door, if you please.'

Aunt Jane had been an obstinate creature from babyhood, and had never obeyed anybody, until she received good reasons therefore; but she was so startled by Madge's tone, that she advanced and closed the door, at once.

Her very unexpected submission restored Madge's composure. She said, quite calmly: "Aunt Jane, you could not have told Mr. Greatorex that I am engaged to my cousin Morton? Please explain! He misunderstood something you said —I do not like it, and Morton would not."

Poor Aunt Jane's presence of mind, for once, deserted her.

"Morton expects— why you know— ever since you were a child," she stammered. Then she caught Hugh's eyes, and grew angry. "You ought to be ashamed of yourself!" She cried. "What do you come here for, trying to make mischief between Madge and me? I never ought to have let you into the house. Oh! Madge, don't mind him— his aunt says he's as bad as he can be; oh! It isn't— oh! You don't—" And Aunt Jane burst out crying, reading such revelations in the faces of the young people, that she lost her head completely.

"I am at a loss to understand what you mean by making mischief, Miss Evans," said Hugh, white and wrathful. "And—"

"Will you please both be silent!" Exclaimed Madge.

"No," said Hugh, obstinately. "I— I am going— I will leave you, ladies."

"I wish you would," moaned Aunt Jane.

"Some explanation of my conduct is due myself," pursued Hugh, with his eyes fixed on Madge. "I had not meant to say a word. I— the truth is— do not be angry— I have learned to love you very dearly, during these weeks. When Miss Evans gave me, yesterday, to understand that you were engaged to your cousin, it opened my eyes. I think I had just been dreaming— I think I will go— I cannot explain— I— I beg your pardon, Miss Madge— I am going."

These last words roused the girl, she turned toward her aunt.

"Be good enough, at least, to tell Mr. Greatorex that he misunderstood you," said she, in an icy tone.

"No such thing!" Groaned the spinster. "I always expected it, so did Morton. Why, he wrote— he will be here in a week. He is coming on purpose to ask you to marry him," sobbed Aunt Jane, bitterly.

"Which I shall not do," cried Madge. "Mr. Greatorex, if you will excuse us, I will say, good morning —my aunt is not well."

"One moment," said Hugh; he had suddenly recovered his composure. "I meant to go without speaking. I have known you too short a time to venture to speak— but I must now— I love you, Madge, I love you!"

"Ain't you ashamed of yourself?" Cried Aunt Jane. "When your own relative says the most dreadful things of you. When— when— oh, Madge! If you don't send him about his business, I'll never forgive you."

She dashed out of the room, so near hysterics that she dared not stop an instant longer. The young pair were alone, free to arrive at an explanation, if they saw fit.

And the spinster had brought about this state of affairs by her own imbecile conduct —she realized that— and it was the only thing she had sanity left to realize as she fled through the hall. She was dashing up the stairs, regardless of the fact that Susan, the housemaid, stood in the outer doorway, holding parley with a woman.

"Miss Evans, here is a person wishes to see you— very particular," called Susan. Miss Jane stopped. "She does not know you, she says, but she wants to see you— very particular."

Miss Jane furtively dried her eyes on a corner of her shawl, and turned towards the vestibule. By Susan's side stood a meek-looking, little, middle-aged woman, dressed in mourning, with an old-fashioned black bonnet on her head, which looked conscious of its shortcomings, and yet had, somehow, an impudent expression, totally at variance with its wearer's appearance, as if it meant to compensate for its defects by an extra amount of assurance.

"You wished to see me?" Asked Aunt Jane.

"Yes, I do," answered the woman, in a voice at once fretful and frightened, though the bonnet was so entirely the prominent thing about her that Miss Evans, in her confused state of mind, had an insane feeling that it was the bonnet which made reply. "I do want to see you. I came on purpose; can I speak to you, ma'am?"

"Of course," said the spinster. She descended the two steps she had mounted, crossed the hall, and opened the door of the library, adding, "Will you walk in here, if you please."

She concluded that the meek stranger had come for advice or help. Aunt Jane was liberal with her money— notably so— and not averse to offering counsel, and very frequently received applications, at least, for the first article, from people she had never seen before, so the woman's visit caused neither her or Susan any surprise.

She led the way into the library, and the belligerent bonnet followed, the woman under it looking as meek as Moses, all the while.

"Pray, sit down," said Aunt Jane, addressing the bonnet. She knew how crazy her feeling was, but she could not overcome it; and in the troubled state of her nerves, the wearer of that head gear seemed of slight consequence, in comparison with the thing itself.

The little woman complied with the request; but she sat on the very edge of her chair, and made Aunt Jane more nervous than ever, for she fully expected to see her tumble off.

"You wanted to see me," at last said the spinster, "I wish you would tell me what I can do for you. I am a little in a hurry;" and it seemed to her as if she must rush off, and end the interview she had so insanely left that youthful couple to enjoy.

"I— I'm sorry to be a trouble," sobbed the woman.

"Oh, it's not the trouble—"

"I— I hadn't maybe a right to come; but I couldn't help it— oh, I couldn't!"

"No, I am sure you could not! There, there, tell me all about it. Lord bless us, don't cry like that!" Exclaimed Aunt Jane, driven nearly out of her senses by contending emotions. "Now, do tell me, that's a good soul— whatever it is, I dare say we can set it right— if— if it's any bother about money—"

"Oh, it's not money!" Broke in the woman. "It's our Emily— the doctor says she'll die, if her mind ain't set at rest. Oh, dear! Oh, dear! It's my sister," she went on, sobbing. "And a prettier creature never lived; and she with more book-learnin' than you could name in a week; and a-dyin'. I tell you, the doctor says she'll die!"

"I am very, very sorry. Anything I can do—"

"Oh, deary me, deary me; I know I'm telling it all wrong end up," sobbed the woman, again. "I couldn't bear it no longer. It was a made-up name and all. But they was lawfully married— we've all the 'stificates— and I found it all out— how he'd been deceiving of us— how that he was at his aun'ts, and all; and I just slipped into the train, and off I came, and when I got there, the hired gal— she said, she was gone—"

"Oh, who was gone?" Cried Aunt Jane, nearly maddened.

"As I'm telling you— Mrs. Lyttimer— but the gal, she know'd all about him, and just how he's been a-going on with your niece, that the neighborhood says he's to marry, and it was likely I'd find him here now, and so on I came— and, oh, ma'am, he's lawfully married to our Emily."

"You will drive me out of my senses, if you do not stop!" Groaned Aunt Jane. "Now, tell me whom you are talking of."

"Just him, I tell you, and tell you, and—"

"Do you mean Mr. Greatorex?" Asked Aunt Jane.

"Of course. Ain't I saying it, and a-saying it?" Sobbed the woman, slipping out of her chair, and sitting, huddled, a helpless heap of misery on the floor, while the black bonnet danced an insane jig over her head.

Aunt Jane rose. A strange, icy wrath stilled the confusion in her brain. It was all plain to her; she needed no further explanations.

"Get up," she said, sternly; "get up, and come with me."

There was such command in her voice, that the woman obeyed at once. Even her tears were checked, and she stood, staring at the spinster, in a kind of imbecile trance of fright. "She'll die! The doctor says our Emily'll die," she whispered, in a faint, husky tone.

"Come with me," repeated Aunt Jane, so completely, body and soul, under the control of that strange, frozen rage, that it was as if she obeyed the command of a spirit, rather than any impulse of her own mind. "Come with me."

She seized the woman's arm, and hurried her, too much frightened for words, along the hall. Aunt Jane threw open the door of the breakfast room; and fairly dragged the woman in; shut the door; and startled the pair standing at the window by exclaiming: "Mr. Hugh Greatorex, here is your wife's sister. She wants you to go home. Your wife is dying."

Miss Jane ended her sentence, and a sudden faintness came over her. She dropped the woman's arm, sank into the nearest chair, and closed her eyes. There was an instant's complete silence, then Miss Jane heard the woman croak: "That ain't Emily's husband. I never set eyes on the man before. Oh! Sir, if so be your name is Greatorex —though you hain't got no family look to him— and if so be you know where he is, speak it out, or you'll have a murder on your soul —yes, you will— I tell you, the doctor says our Emily'll die — she'll die!"

Miss Jane could not open her eyes, or speak; the little woman's voice had risen to a shrill cry and cut the spinster's ears like a knife. She was conscious that Madge and Hugh had gone up to the woman, and were trying to comfort the poor creature; but Miss Jane herself could only sit helpless and dumb. Then she heard Hugh's voice.

"I think you mistook me for my cousin, Harvey," he said.

"That's your name —I mean his— but I'm so worn out, I don't know nothing," moaned the woman in black. "Only, I never set eyes on you before —only I'm sure your very good, and the young lady, too. And, oh! If so be you have any mercy on our Emily, do tell me where to find him; for she'll die, the doctor says, unless I bring him."

It was a long while before the woman could be quieted; but when she was restored, the explanation proved easy enough.

Miss Jane had confused Mrs. Lyttimer's account, concerning the two cousins, and had put all Harvey's sins on Hugh's shoulders.

Perhaps, you will like to know, that poor Emily did not die. Hugh went in search of his cousin, and took him to his wife, and they say, Harvey repented, and made a tolerable husband, as such uncomfortable possessions go. I hope so, I am sure.

A very unpleasant task devolved upon Aunt Jane; that of writing to Morton Walsh, and telling him that he might spare himself the trouble of a journey, at least on Madge's account. Morton was very indignant at first —then very sorry for Madge, and later, he sent her a wedding present, accompanied by a letter of pitying counsel, at which Aunt Jane laughed harder than anybody.

Madge and Hugh were married in the autumn. Mrs. Crowe learned of the event in advance, and appeared at the house in due season, basket, Blowsey and all, to state her views.

"My dear," she said. "Excusin' the freedom —it's all along o' them —o' them roses. And when you're married, you shall have more, the finest I can get at this season. Garden roses is not, nor crociases neither, but you'll have chrysanthemummers, and geraniannas in beauchiful abundiance, and so I tells you clearly; and, oh! Such real Boston beauties of roses as I'll bring!"

She kept her word, and the old mansion was a pretty sight, one glorious morning; and Aunt Jane the happiest elderly spinster you ever set eyes on.

—*Peterson's Magazine*, December, 1877, pp. 398—405.

Index of Poem Titles

Index of First Lines

About the Editor

Sarah A. Chrisman is the author of the charming Tales of Chetzemoka historical fiction series as well as *This Victorian Life*, *Victorian Secrets*, and others. She lives in a house built in 1888, sews her own clothes, bakes her own bread in a wood-burning stove, and incorporates as many elements of Victorian culture and technology into her daily life as humanly possible. To learn more about Sarah and her books, go to www.ThisVictorianLife.com.

The Tales of Chetzemoka
By Sarah A. Chrisman

In a seaport town in the late 19th-century Pacific Northwest, a group of friends find themselves drawn together —by chance, by love, and by the marvelous changes their world is undergoing. In the process, they learn that the family we choose can be just as important as the ones we're born into. Join their adventures in
The Tales of Chetzemoka!
http://www.thisvictorianlife.com/ historical-fiction.html

First Wheel in Town
http://www.thisvictorianlife.com/first-wheel-in-town.html

Love Will Find A Wheel
http://www.thisvictorianlife.com/love-will-find-a-wheel.html

A Rapping At The Door
http://www.thisvictorianlife.com/a-rapping-at-
the-door.html

Delivery Delayed
http://www.thisvictorianlife.com/delivery-
delayed.html

A Trip and a Tumble
http://www.thisvictorianlife.com/a-trip-and-a-
tumble.html

Made in the USA
Middletown, DE
26 March 2019